THE SCIENCE CLUB
INVESTIGATES
THE HUMAN BODY

By Mary Auld
Illustrated by Sernur Işik

WAYLAND

The Science Club is busy investigating when Jiang's front tooth falls out! He proudly shows the other children, but Ava notices blood on Jiang's lip.

Mrs Khan is calm. "It happens sometimes when a tooth comes out. Jiang just needs to rinse out his mouth with water. The bleeding will have stopped by then. The human body is amazing! It can get better all by itself."

"How does that happen?" asks Jiang. "How does the human body work?"

After Jiang has washed, Mrs Khan begins. "Let's start with how the human body works. The body has lots of different parts, inside and out, that work together. It's like a machine. Help me name the outside parts."

"You stand on your feet and legs," says Liam. "And you sit on your bottom," says Ava, "bending your back and tummy."

"Next come your chest and shoulders," says Jack. "They join to your arms and hands," continues Emily. "And your neck connects with your head," adds Winston.

Mrs Khan asks them to link some outside parts to their senses.

Mrs Khan claps, but adds an interesting fact: "All your skin is sensitive to touch. It feels heat and cold too. Your skin is an organ, the largest in your body. It protects your body inside and out."

"Let's look under the skin next, starting with Stanley – our very own skeleton!" says Mrs Khan.

The Club loves the classroom skeleton. His plastic bones are made to be like the bones in their bodies.
"The skeleton gives our bodies shape," says Ava.
"And lets us move," adds Jiang.

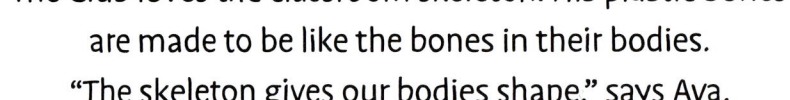

As the children move Stanley, Mrs Khan explains how the bones inside our bodies are moved by muscles.

"Muscles are joined to our bones by bands called tendons," she says.

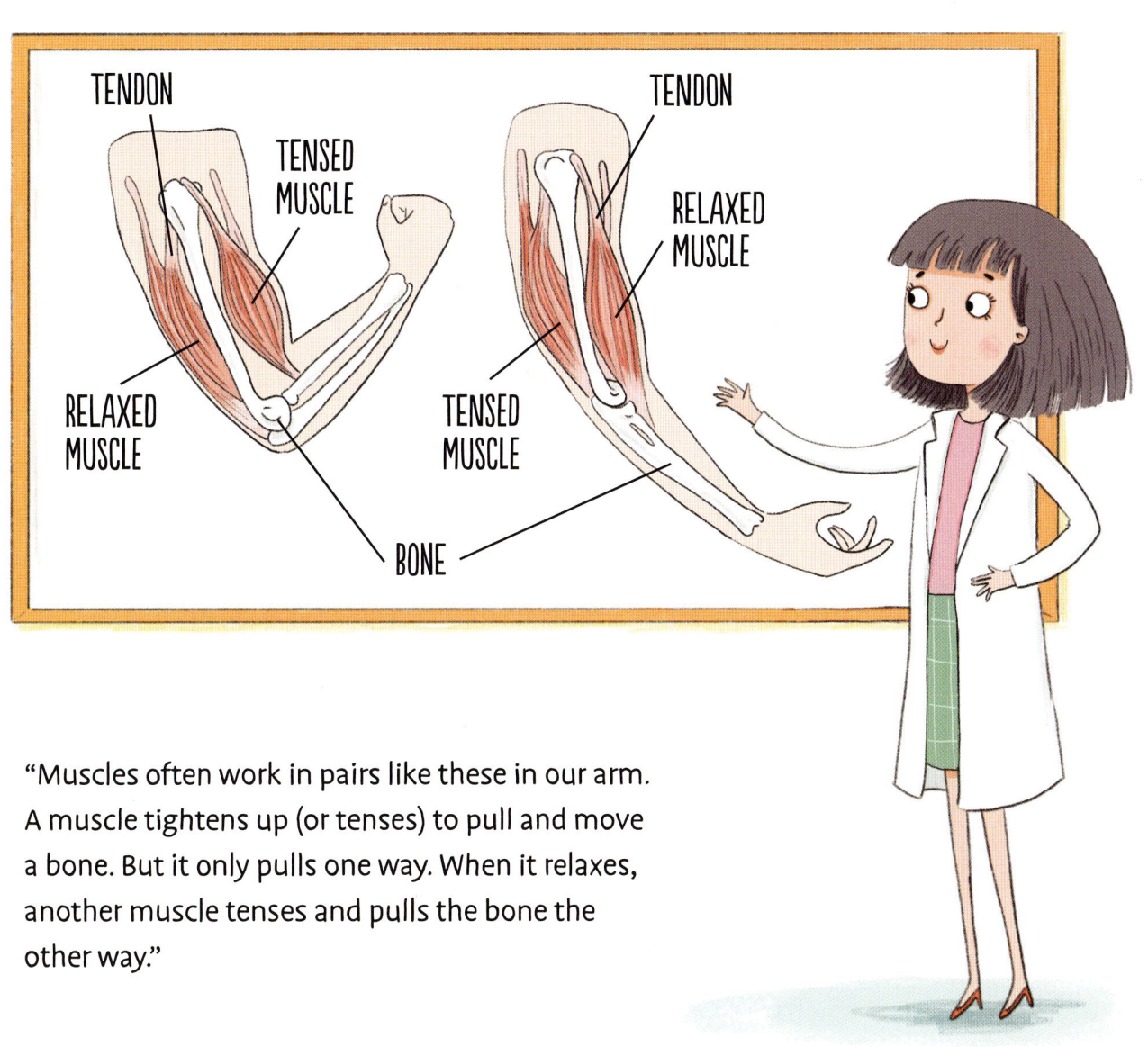

"Muscles often work in pairs like these in our arm. A muscle tightens up (or tenses) to pull and move a bone. But it only pulls one way. When it relaxes, another muscle tenses and pulls the bone the other way."

"What other job does our skeleton do?" asks Mrs Khan.
"Think what's inside your hard skull!" she adds.
"Your brain is in your skull," says Hazim. "Your skeleton protects the parts inside your body!"

"Well done, Hazim," congratulates Mrs Khan. "Those parts are organs too, like your skin. Your brain is your thinking organ. Nerves carry signals to and from your brain to the rest of your body. What do your ribs protect?"
"Your heart?" says Zoey.
Mrs Khan takes a deep breath.
"Oh, and your lungs!"
adds Zoey.

"Brilliant!" claps Mrs Khan. "Your heart pumps blood around your body and your lungs breathe air in and out."

She puts up a poster. "There are more organs. Most are linked to digestion – how we break up our food. And our teeth help with that, too. Jiang may find chewing a little difficult for a while!"

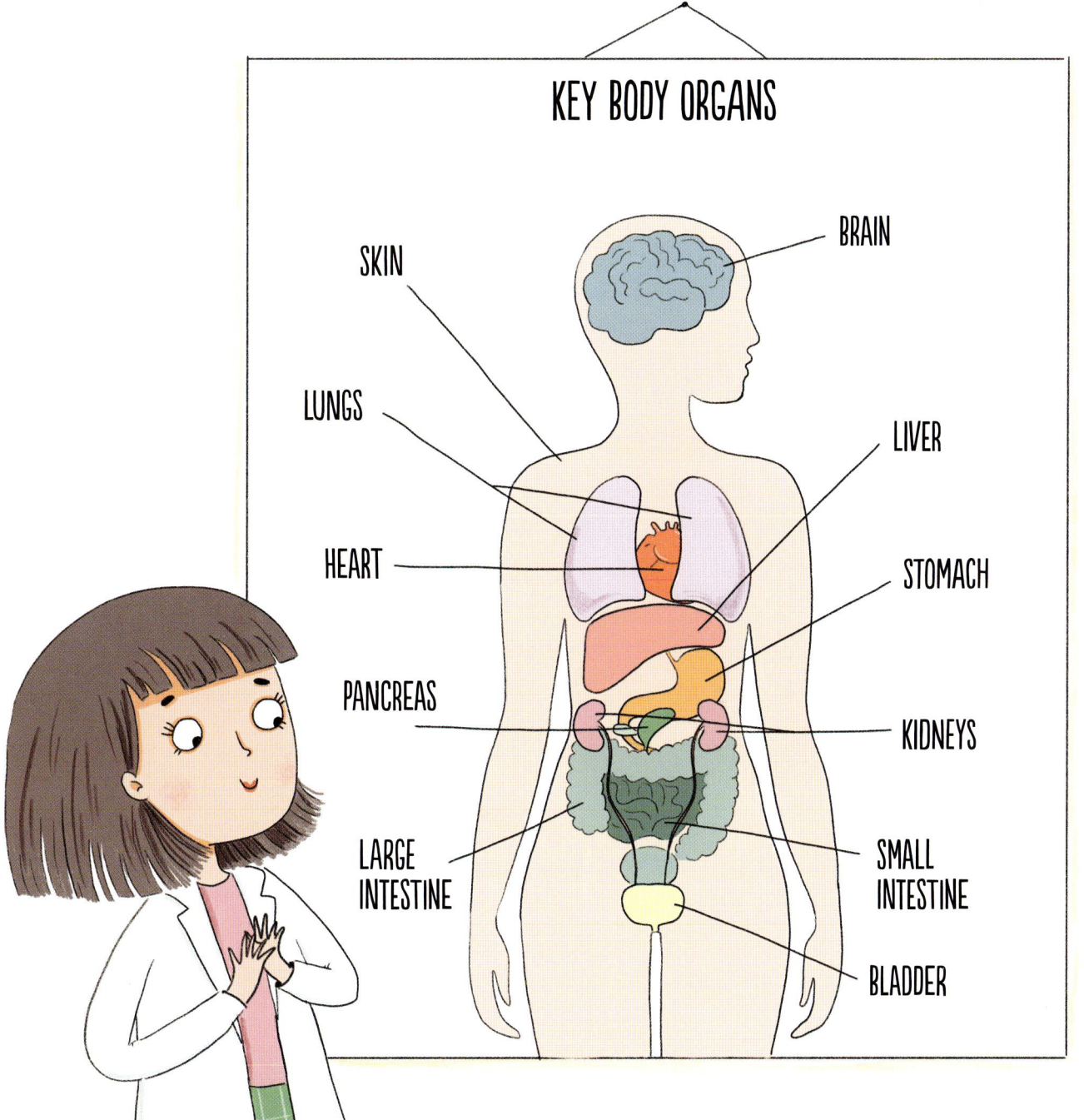

"Why do we need to eat?" asks Jiang. "Your body needs food to work," says Mrs Khan. "Why do you think that is?"
"Mum tells me to eat up because food is my body's fuel," says Paola. "It gives you energy!"

"'Then your body needs something else to take the energy out of the food – oxygen," says Mrs Khan. "What's oxygen and how do we get it?"
"Oxygen is one of the gases in air!" remembers Hazim. "We breathe it into our lungs!" adds Zoey.

"And there's a third thing we need," says Mrs Khan. "It is in every part of your body. It makes up half your body weight, but it needs replacing."

"Water!" shouts Ava.

"Exactly," laughs Mrs Khan. "All plants and animals need water, food and oxygen to live."

The Club wants to find out more but it's time to go home.
"Can you bring back your tooth next week, Jiang?" asks Mrs Khan.

AT THE NEXT CLUB, Mrs Khan has some healthy snacks ready. "These will help us investigate how we digest food," she explains. "First we'll look at teeth."
"I can't crunch on a carrot with my front tooth missing," complains Jiang.

PREMOLARS crush
INCISORS cut
CANINES tear
MOLARS grind

"You can have cheese and tomato sandwiches," says Ava.
"Yes, humans can eat a variety of foods – and it's healthy to mix them up," agrees Mrs Khan.

"Einstein can have Jiang's carrot," Nadia suggests.
"His teeth are very good for crunching!"
"Good observation!" says Mrs Khan. "Let's INVESTIGATE our teeth and compare them with other animals."

The children look at Jiang's tooth and then Stanley the skeleton's full set. They research Einstein the hamster's teeth and other animals' teeth.
"Animals' teeth are adapted to what they eat!" reads Ava.

Next, the children tuck into their snacks as Mrs Khan talks. "Imagine you've shrunk to fit into a mini explorer pod hidden in a sandwich. We'll take a trip through the digestive system."

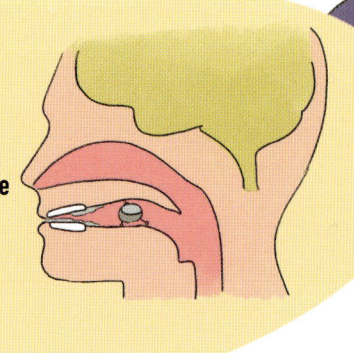

1. We start off in the mouth. Teeth chop up the sandwich. The taste triggers extra spit — or saliva. It makes the food wet and smooth — ready to swallow.

4. Now we go into the large intestine with the remaining mush. This fatter tube is full of helpful bacteria.

The bacteria take out more goodness from food to give to the body. The large intestine takes out more water, too.

"The pod won't visit the kidneys. They aren't part of the digestive system but they are important," adds Mrs Khan. "Kidneys take out things the body doesn't need, including some water, and send them to the bladder. They come out when you wee."

2. Now the tongue pushes us and the food down the throat and into a muscle-lined tube, which squeezes it to the stomach. The stomach churns up the food with digestive juices to make a liquid mush.

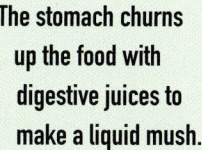

3. We float inside the mush into the small intestine — a coiled tube over 6 metres long. Juices from the pancreas mix into the food mush, while the sides take out water and food goodness for the body to use.

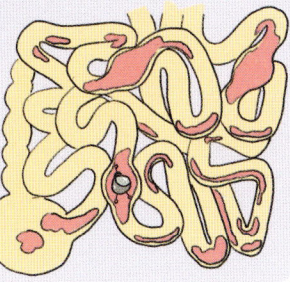

5. We are near the end of the large intestine now. Welcome to the rectum!

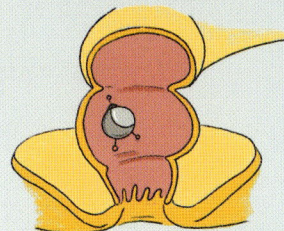

Our pod is surrounded by soft but solid food waste — poo! Our digestive journey will soon be over.

"Shall I go and look for the pod in the toilet?" asks Winston.

Jack has another question. "What is the goodness from food?"
"The goodness is made up of nutrients, including the energy from food, and other things your body needs, such as Vitamin C or calcium," says Mrs Khan. "Vitamin C helps you fight infections like colds."

"Calcium helps make your teeth and bones strong."

"How do the nutrients go around the body?" asks Emily.

"They are carried in your blood," replies Mrs Khan. "There's a network of tubes, or vessels, that carries blood to every little part of your body."
"And your heart pushes your blood around," remembers Zoey.

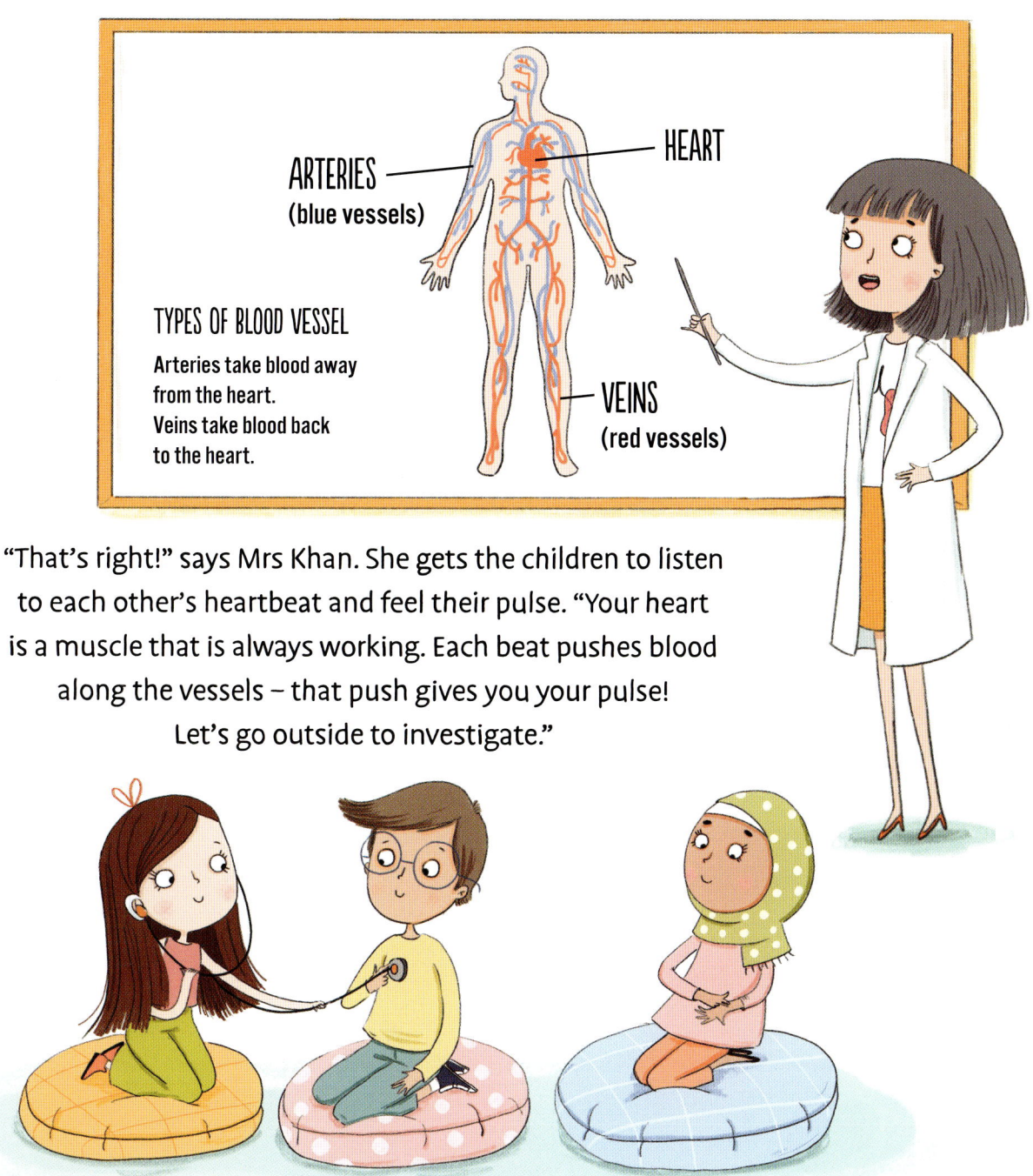

ARTERIES (blue vessels)

HEART

VEINS (red vessels)

TYPES OF BLOOD VESSEL
Arteries take blood away from the heart.
Veins take blood back to the heart.

"That's right!" says Mrs Khan. She gets the children to listen to each other's heartbeat and feel their pulse. "Your heart is a muscle that is always working. Each beat pushes blood along the vessels – that push gives you your pulse! Let's go outside to investigate."

"Take deep breaths. Feel your lungs get bigger and smaller," says Mrs Khan. "Your lungs are lined with lots of tiny blood vessels. These take the oxygen you breathe into your blood."

"The nutrients in your blood combine with the oxygen to let your body use its food energy. This changes the oxygen into carbon dioxide. Your blood carries that back to your lungs for you to breathe out."

"Carbon dioxide is another gas in air," remembers Hazim.

AT THE NEXT CLUB, Jiang is pleased. "The tooth fairy gave me £2!" he says. "And my new tooth is coming through."
"It should last you for the rest of your life," Ava says.
"Humans and other animals all grow and change – it's part of their life cycle – but they do it in different ways," says Mrs Khan.

"Einstein the hamster was fully grown at 12 weeks. You could be in your twenties before you are fully grown."

The children draw different stages of the human life cycle and take Mrs Khan through it.

"Well done," says Mrs Khan. "We call the time between child and adult 'adolescence'. That's when you grow a lot and your body changes, ready to have babies. It can start before you are a teenager."

The Club keeps talking. "Adult means when you are fully grown," says Jack.
"And old age is when you die," adds Paola.
"No, people can die before that," says Nadia, hotly.

Mrs Khan joins in. "Nadia and Jack are both right. As you get older, your body gets worn out and stops working so well – and you do eventually die. But, very sadly, things can happen at any stage in the human life cycle that make your body stop."

Everyone knows that Nadia's mum has died. They feel sad.
Paola gives Nadia a hug.

After a moment, Mrs Khan starts to talk again. "But often if you get ill or have an accident, your body makes you better. Think how Jiang's mouth stopped bleeding – tiny parts in the blood block up a cut. They form a scab. You can see one on Winston's knee."

"My bone mended when I broke my arm," remembers Hazim.

"And we get better after a cold," adds Zoey.

"Your body machine can repair itself," confirms Mrs Khan.
"But sometimes it needs some help. If you have an infection,
you may need medicine to make it better. Doctors look at broken
bones with x-rays and decide what help they need to mend
properly. For example, they put Hazim's arm in a plaster cast."

"But you also need to look after your body
so it doesn't go wrong!" Mrs Khan adds.
"Exercise keeps you healthy. Drinking lots of
water and getting plenty of sleep helps too.
So does keeping clean – you wash away dirt
and germs that can make you ill."

"You need to eat healthy food," adds Ava. "Like green vegetables. Although it's okay to have cake too sometimes."

"Well said, Ava," agrees Mrs Khan. "Let's INVESTIGATE what goes into making a healthy diet. And we can finish our project by all thinking of some healthy lifestyle changes."

JOIN THE SCIENCE CLUB

INVESTIGATE different types of teeth in humans and other animals (see page 12–13). You will need: reference books, internet access, a printer, scissors, pens and paper.

1. Draw (or print out) a set of human teeth (see page 12) and label them.

2. Research our four different kinds of teeth. Why do you think we need them? How do they help us eat? Write your answers around your picture.

3. Choose some other animals to research. Take one from each of the following groups: (A) sheep, cows, antelope (B) rabbit, hamster, agouti (C) dog, brown bear, baboon (D) domestic cat, lion.

4. Draw a grid with four rows (one for each of your animal choices) and three columns. In first column, draw or stick a picture of the animal. Use the second column for an image of their teeth.

5. In the last column, note each animal's diet and how their teeth are adapted to it. Decide if they are herbivores (plant-eaters), omnivores (meat- and plant-eaters) or carnivores (meat-eaters). Which group do humans go in?

INVESTIGATE what makes a healthy human diet (see page 25).
Use your research to plan and make a picnic. You will need: reference books, internet access, paper and pens. You will also need the ingredients and equipment to make your picnic – and some adult help.

1. Research what humans need to have a balanced, healthy diet. Look at the different food groups and don't forget drinks.

2. Make notes and draw a diagram to show a balanced diet: for example, a plate divided into different sized sections for the different food groups, and how much you need of each one.

3. Now plan a healthy picnic lunch, with sandwiches, drinks and some snacks. What sort of bread will you use? What will you put inside your sandwiches? What sweet treat might you include?

4. Get together the ingredients of your picnic, make it and eat it! Ask an adult to help with any shopping or if you need to use sharp knives.

GLOSSARY

adapted	Changed to suit something, such as the food available in a place
bacteria	Tiny living things far too small to see without a microscope
bladder	The stretchy bag-like organ attached to our kidneys that holds our wee
blood	The red liquid that carries nutrients and energy to different parts of our body and takes away waste
brain	The organ that controls our body and how it works
carbon dioxide	One of the gases in air. People breathe out carbon dioxide
digestion	The way we break up our food to take out its nutrients
digestive system	The different parts of the body that work together to digest our food
energy	What enables things to work, change and move. There are different forms of energy, including heat, light and food, and they can change from one form to another
heart	The muscular organ that pumps blood around the body all the time
joint	Where two bones connect, letting us move our skeleton
kidneys	The pair of organs that take out waste and water we do not need from the blood
large intestine	Part of the digestive system, this organ removes water from our digested food, leaving the waste that makes our poo
liver	One of the organs that helps clean the blood. It also produces the digestive juices used by the stomach to break up our food
lungs	The two stretchy, bag-like organs we use for breathing
muscles	Parts of the body made of bundles of fibres that let our body move and work
nerves	The network of long, thin fibres, a bit like electrical wires, that connects your brain to the rest of your body, carrying messages between them
nutrients	The parts, or goodness, of our food that we need to make our body work
organ	A part of the body that performs a particular job
oxygen	One of the gases in air. Humans and other animals need oxygen to breathe
pancreas	The organ in our digestive system which supplies digestive juices to the small intestine. It also helps ensure the right levels of food energy in our blood

skeleton The hard, inner frame of our body made up of bones

skin The large organ that covers our body and is sensitive to touch

small intestine One of the organs of the digestive system. It takes nutrients and water from our food, passing them into the blood

stomach One of the organs of the digestive system, where chewed-up food is mixed with digestive juices to make a mush our body can digest

vitamins One of the nutrients in food that help our body work. For example, vitamins help our body fight disease and build strong bones

FURTHER INFORMATION

Here are some other books about the human body you might like to read:

Boom! Science: Human Body by Georgia Amson-Bradshaw (Wayland, 2019)
Look Inside: What Happens When You Eat? Emily Bone (Usborne, 2019)
Step into Science: The Body by Peter Riley (Franklin Watts, 2023)
My Very Important Human Body Encyclopedia (DK Children, 2023)

Check out these websites:

www.bbc.co.uk/bitesize/topics/z7x78xs
A selection of fun videos and activities exploring the human body.
www.youtube.com/watch?v=dhpCdqOtujo
Learn about Healthy Habits from this 'Wellbeing for Children' video

WARNING

Do not put your body in danger. For example, do not play near water or traffic without an adult. Do not pick up things with sharp edges, such as broken glass. Get adult help to wash a cut and keep it clean afterwards.

SAFETY PRECAUTIONS

Always work with an adult while doing the investigations in this book. Do not go to the shops without an adult. Always wash your hands when preparing food and ask for adult help cutting things. Keep surfaces clean and clear up afterwards.

INDEX

adolescence 21
arms 4, 7, 23, 24

back 4
bacteria 14
bladder 9, 14
blood 2, 3, 9, 17, 18, 19, 23
blood vessels 17, 18
bones 6, 7, 16, 23, 24
bottom 4
brain 8, 9

carbon dioxide 18

digestion 9, 12, 14, 15

energy 10, 16, 18, 19

feet 4
food 9, 10, 11, 12, 14, 15, 16, 18, 25

hands 4, 27
heart 8, 9, 17, 19

joints 6

kidneys 9, 14

large intestine 9, 14, 15
legs 4, 9
life cycle 20, 21, 22
liver 9
lungs 8, 9, 10, 18, 19

mouth 3, 5, 14, 23
muscles 7, 15, 17, 19
neck 4
nerves 8
nutrients 16, 18

organs 5, 8, 9

oxygen 10, 11, 18, 19

pancreas 9, 14, 15
pulse 17, 19

ribs 8

skeleton 6, 8, 13
skin 5, 6, 8, 9
skull 8
small intestine 9, 14, 15
stomach 9, 14, 15

teeth 2, 3, 9, 12, 13, 14, 16, 20, 26, 27
tendons 7
throat 14, 15
tummy 4, 20

vitamins 16

water 3, 11, 14, 15, 24, 26

First published in Great Britain in 2025 by Wayland
Copyright © Hodder and Stoughton, 2025

All rights reserved.

Wayland, an imprint of Hachette Children's Group
Part of Hodder and Stoughton
Carmelite House, 50 Victoria Embankment, London EC4Y 0DZ

An Hachette UK Company
www.hachette.co.uk
www.hachettechildrens.co.uk

HB ISBN: 978 1 5263 2161 9
PB ISBN: 978 1 5263 2160 2

Design by Clare Mills
Edited by Julia Bird and Rachel Cooke
Science consultancy by Peter Riley

Printed in China

The authorised representative in the EEA is Hachette Ireland, 8 Castlecourt Centre, Dublin 15, D15 XTP3, Ireland (email: info@hbgi.ie)

Note to parents and teachers: every effort has been made by the Publishers to ensure websites are suitable for children, that they are of the highest educational value, and that they contain no inappropriate or offensive material. However, because of the nature of the Internet, it is impossible to guarantee that the contents of these sites will not be altered. We strongly advise that Internet access is supervised by a responsible adult.